A WAKE FOR THE LIVING

A WAKE FOR THE LIVING

Radmila Lazić

Translated from the Serbian by Charles Simic

Graywolf Press
SAINT PAUL, MINNESOTA

Publication of this volume is made possible in part by a grant provided by the Minnesota State Arts Board, through an appropriation by the Minnesota State Legislature; a grant from the Wells Fargo Foundation Minnesota; and a grant from the National Endowment for the Arts. Significant support has also been provided by the Bush Foundation; Target, Marshall Field's and Mervyn's with support from the Target Foundation; the McKnight Foundation; and other generous contributions from foundations, corporations, and individuals. To these organizations and individuals we offer our heartfelt thanks.

NATIONAL
ENDOWMENT
FOR THE ARTS

MINNESOTA
STATE ARTS BOARD

A Lannan Translation Selection
Funding the translation and publication of exceptional literary works

The poems in this collection come from the original Serbian publications: *Price i Druge Pesme* (KOV, 1998), *Iz Anamneze* (RAD, 2000), and *Doroti Parker–Bluz* (in manuscript).

Some of these translations have previously appeared in the following magazines, to whose editors grateful acknowledgment is made: *Circumference*, *Field*, *Jubilat*, and *Verse*.

Published by Graywolf Press
2402 University Avenue, Suite 203
Saint Paul, Minnesota 55114

www.graywolfpress.org

Published in the United States of America

ISBN 1-55597-390-6

2 4 6 8 9 7 5 3 1
First Graywolf Printing, 2003

Library of Congress Control Number: 2003101173

Cover design: Steven Rachwal

Cover art: Digital Vision/Getty Images

CONTENTS

THREE

INTRODUCTION: TRANSLATING RADMILA LAZIĆ

With a few exceptions, I have only translated poets I have admired deeply. More than that, they were poets who could do things I was unable to do myself as a poet. It was almost an act of envy I was engaged in. I imagined that I was writing the poem I was in the process of translating. Poets have often regarded themselves as mediums, mouthpieces for the Muse, so why should that not be true of translators?

This leads me to Radmila Lazić, whose poems I have been working on recently. What moved me immediately when I first read her, and forced my hand, as it were, is her uncommon eloquence. This ability is rarely found in poetry and equally infrequently in life. I have in mind someone finding appropriate words, words that strike home in a tragic or a happy moment. We all know that we live in a particular never-to-be-repeated historical moment, but how do we find words to say what we only feel and do not recognize until someone else has said it? As we see from Lazić's poetry, that may be one of the noblest roles of the poet.

Eloquence, of course, is an art of persuasion. Being an art, it has its bag of tricks that comes out of the poetry of the past. If Lazić speaks eloquently, it is because she has heard how authentic poetry speaks. In other words, she knows the difference between empty rhetoric and words that make one heart move closer to another. Can a lyric poem tell the truth? Can a song? You bet they can.

What is also worth noting about Lazić is how rich in detail her poems are. What memorable imagery and figures of speech she has! Almost every one of her lines is a surprise, an unexpected imaginative turn. It's because she's both out to break taboos and to keep the tradition of women's lyric poetry going. "I, too, dislike it," our great poet, Marianne Moore, said of poetry. Every institution and every art needs a little irreverence from time to time to keep them alive.

I believe a few of Radmila Lazić's poems belong with the very best of Serbian poetry. Translating her, I was also reminded how intelligent a poet has to be. Despite what people may think, lyric poetry requires extraordinary intelligence, because the poet—or rather, each poem—has to construct its own metaphysics, some sense of heaven and hell to go along with everything else that's happening in that poem. What I like about Radmila Lazić's poems is that she doesn't forget anything, including us readers. It does not surprise me at all that she translates so well and that she sounds so terrific in English.

Charles Simic

ONE

SMAKNUĆA

Kasno se rodih, i s viškom godina,
Moj Hamlete,
Da bih bila bubuljičava Ofelija.

Da svoju kosu kao poleglo žito
Rasprostrem po tamnim vodama.
Da svojim plutajućim očima
Uznemirim plutajuće lokvanje.

Da skliznem među ribe ribi nalik.
Da kao mrtva školjka ne dno padnem.
Da se zarijem u pesak kraj ljubavnih olupina,
Ja amfora, da se spletem međ morske trave.

Radije bih da mi haljinu skineš,
Nek mi kraj nogu padne kao lišće s jasike—
Koju vetar namah i ne pitajući stresa,
Kao da ne čini ništa.

Radije bih to smaknuće.
Večnost tvojih ruku na mom vratu.

DEATH SENTENCES

I was born too late and I am much too old,
My dear Hamlet,
To be your pimply Ophelia,

To let my hair like flattened wheat
Spread over the dark waters
And upset the floating water lilies
With my floating eyes,

To glide fishlike between fishes,
Sink to the bottom like a dead seashell,
Burrow in sand next to shipwrecks of love,
I, the amphora, entangled in seaweeds.

I'd rather you take off my dress,
Let it fall at my feet like aspen leaves
The wind shakes without permission
As if there's nothing to it.

I'd rather have that death sentence:
Eternity of your arms around my neck.

IZ MOG «CAREVANJA»

Po Adamu Zagajevskom

Istorija samoće je duga.
Sastoji se od niza pojedinačnih,
Nalik jedna drugoj kao travka travci.
A opet svaka u svom srcu ima
Svoga miša ili krticu.
Svaka govori jednim od mrtvih jezika.
Kao jezero što govori svojom ćutnjom.
Istina je negde tu.
Prikrada se kao sumraci
Izmedju drevnih stabala.
Koja se čine kao ljudi.
Ali oni su odsutni.
Nečim zabavljeni.
Dobro je što je tako.
Mogu da se okrenem
I vidim šumu kako za mnom korača,
Nogu pred nogu kao mesečar u snu.
Biva to pred zoru,
Dok se pramenje magle,
Koju zovemo izmaglica,
Puši i diže prema suncu.
Ostaju samo prorezi,
Iskidane zavese,
Kroz koje se može proći
S onu stranu,
Po svoj životopis.
Dok stabla još sanjaju
I trava sanja.
Biva kao na javi.
Bez jadanja.

FROM MY "KINGDOM"

To Adam Zagajewski

The history of solitude is long.
It's made up of a string of individuals
That resemble one another like blades of grass,
And still each one in its heart
Has a mouse or a mole.
Each speaks one of the dead languages
The way a lake speaks with its silence.
The truth is to be found somewhere thereabouts,
It sneaks upon us like nightfall
Between the ancient trees
That give the appearance of being human beings
But they are absent,
Busy with something else.
It's good the way it is now.
I can turn and see the forest
Walking after me step by step
Like a sleepwalker in a dream
That happens toward daybreak
When the patches of fog one calls mist
Burn and rise toward the sun.
There are only slits left,
Ripped curtains
Through which it is possible to pass
From the other side,
To get hold of one's memoirs
While the trees still dream
And the grass dreams.
It's like one were awake
With nothing to cry over.

DOROTI PARKER—BLUZ

Nevoljena. Nemažena dugo.
Zaboravljena kao rublje na žici.
Ni ludača ni štreberka.
Zarđale pice, postriženog koječega—
Tebe želim sada.
Tebe koga još nisam srela.

Oblačim crne gaćice,
Prekrivam još neolinjalu ćubu.
Mažem usne, pirlitam kosu,
Na štikle se penjem.
Spremna sam za tebe.
Još samo usku haljinu da obučem,
Pa da pretrneš,
Da ti se noge odseku,
Kada me ugledaš takvu.

Srešćemo se slučajno—namerno
Tamo gde jedino mogu biti,
Tamo kuda inače ne idu takvi kao ti.
A takav mi treba, takav ti,
Koji će me odmah povesti kod sebe
Znajući zašto to čini.

Nisu mi potrebne nikakve žvake,
Tipa: jesi li čitala tog i tog?
Da ti pustim klasiku ili bluz?
Toga se naslušah,
Ko vremenske prognoze i tačnog vremena.

Nego da pređem na stvar:
Dajem ti vizu
Za moje telo—moju domovinu.

DOROTHY PARKER BLUES

Unloved. Long uncaressed.
Forgotten like washing on the line.
Neither a mad woman nor a go-getter
With my dry nooky, my sheared something,
It's you I want now,
You whom I've never met.

I'm putting on my black panties,
Covering my still-hairy crotch.
I paint my lips, fluff my hair,
Climb on a pair of heels.
I'm ready for you.
Now I just have to squeeze into a tight dress
To make you gasp,
Have your heart skip a beat
When you see me like that.

We'll meet by chance—intentionally
There where my kind can be found,
Where men like you don't usually go.
That's the type I need, a fellow
Who'll take me home right away
Knowing what he wants to do with me.

I don't need any preliminaries.
Like: Have you read so and so?
Would you like to hear something classical
Or do you prefer the blues?
Like weather forecasts and announcements of correct time—
I've heard them all before.

Let me get to the nitty-gritty:
I give you the visa

Nekad dobro parče,
Ni sad nisam za bacanje.
Koža mi je iznutra plišana,
Kao u perunike.
Pomiriši. Probaj.
Čim zaključaš vrata
Stisni me uz njih,
I počni da me ljubiš
Sve niže i niže.
Ako to ne učiniš ti, učiniću ja.
Moje do maločas zimsko telo
Sad je grm pun divljih pčela.

Poćerdah štošta.
Al sad znam što znam:
Dvanaesti je čas, hvata me frka.
Brzim stigle godine
Natovarene svakojakim prtljagom.
Još romansa ili dve, i poneki flert,
Pa u starudije ili antikvitet.

Ti si mi potreban šećeru,
Dajem ti šansu.
Potri, precrtaj!
Kao kredu sa školske table,
Obriši dane tmurne i dane prazne.
Tu gde sam stavila tačku
Dopiši šta treba.
Otključaj gde bejah zamandaljena.

Ne treba mi nikakvo piće,
Nikakva muzika, ni bla-bla-bla.
Ono što hoću to je dobra ševa.

To my body—my homeland,
Once a good piece of ass,
Even now not to be discarded.
My skin is velvet on the inside,
Like iris.
Smell it. Taste it.
The moment you lock the door
Press me against it
And start kissing me
Lower and lower.
If you won't do it to me, I'll do it to you.
My body, so wintry a moment ago,
Is now a bush full of wild bees.

I squandered this and that
But now I know what I know.
It's high time—I'm in a panic.
My years rode an express train
Loaded with all kinds of luggage,
A romance or two, an occasional flirt,
Then it's off to the old-clothes shop.

You are the one I need, sugar.
I'm offering you a chance,
Rub, cross out
The chalk marks on a blackboard,
Wipe my gloomy days, my empty days.
Add a few needed words,
Unlock me where I was bolted.

I don't need a drink.
No music, no sweet talk.
What I want is a good fuck

Mrak ili svetlo, svejedno.
Ispisujem svoj život sat po sat.
Fućka mi se za tuđe priče, torokanja,
Ćef mi je da grabim i grebem,
Kao ona mačka na limenom krovu
Usijanom od želja.

O, ne umem da držim jezik za zubima,
Mnogo brbljam, kevćem, o ličnim stvarima.

In the dark or with the lights on—it doesn't matter.
I'm writing my life hour by hour.
I don't care about other people's stories.
I like to grab and scratch
Like that cat on a hot tin roof
Sizzling with desire.

Oh, I don't know how to hold my tongue.
I talk too much, yelp about things best kept private.

SMEJAĆU SE SVUDA, PLAKAĆU GDE STIGNEM

Govore da sam lakomislena,
Da mnogo zujim i zunzaram.
Da ne marim za rad i red.
Da bazam i landaram,
Da na sedeljkama osvanjivam,
Da se danju unanokolo vozikam,
Da s nogu džin ispijam,
Da tako i piskaram.
Govore da sam brbljiva,
Da povazdan toročem,
Da jezikom kao zmija palacam.
Da mi ga već jednom treba otfikariti.
Da me treba po njušci zveknuti.
Da me treba ko muvu prikucati.
Govore da mora da imam dobra «leda»
Kad ne prezam ni od čega.
Govore da sam namiguša,
Da flertujem bez pardona
Sa tuđim momcima i muževima,
A da mi i žene nisu mrske.
Jedna opajdara i jedna kuja pričaju
Da šetam žutokljunce a da matorce čerupam,
Da nikom ništa ne dajem za džabe.
Govore da sam prolupala,
Da se na sav glas smejem,
Da se cerekam kao da sam šenula,
Ako mi šta nije po volji
Da plačem kao trogodišnje dete,
Gde god da se zateknem.
A ja im kažem,
Smejaću se svuda, plakaću gde stignem.
Život je kandirano voće & ocat,
U stihove ih umećem u jednakim dozama.

I'LL LAUGH EVERYWHERE, WEEP WHEREVER I CAN

They say I'm easy to fool.
That I buzz like a bumblebee.
That I don't care for work and order.
That I roam around and waste my time.
That I greet dawn at all-night parties.
That I spend my days joyriding.
That I drink gin standing up.
That I scribble poems that way too.
They say I talk too much.
That I beat my gums all day long.
That my tongue flickers like that of a snake.
That it's time for someone to cut it off.
That I could use a punch in the mouth.
That I ought to be pinned like a fly.
They say I must have protection
To go around behaving this way.
They say that I'm a tease.
That I flirt shamelessly with other people's
Lovers and husbands.
That even doing it with a woman is not hateful to me.
Some floozy and some bitch are telling everybody
That I take young boys for a walk
And pluck feathers out of doddering old men.
That I never give any of it for free.
They say that I've gone soft in the head.
That I laugh as if I had a screw loose
If something doesn't please me.
That I sob like a three-year-old child
Wherever I find myself to be.
And I tell them in turn,
I'll laugh everywhere, weep wherever I can.
Life is candied fruit and vinegar,
I add them to my verses in equal amounts.

Moja je sintaksa štimovanje orgulja u venama.
Gorim sa srcem od 500W,
Istina, ne grejem, ali mogu da opečem,
Srcem kao i jezikom—
Koga ne perem i ne stružem Vimom,
Al što zgotovim to i kusam redovno.
Toliko puta se oprljih, a ne zaceli niko.
Ipak, nisam riba na suvom,
Iako na suvom pecam muškarce,
Krajičkom oka, dužinom suknje.
Somići tovljeni požudom
Tu su da bi ih neko ćapio.
Što i činim, ne odričem.
Ali ni ne hajem, za sve te trice i kučine,
Što se oko moga imena spliću
Kao u plićaku čkalj oko trske.
Iznad mene je nebo, u njega gledam,
U zvezde rasute, koje ne mogu skupiti,
Niti hoću.
Nek se umnožavaju.
Nek se pare i nek se umnožavaju,
Neka bude tako.

My syntax is like the tuning of an organ inside the veins.
I burn with a heart 500W strong.
The truth is, I can't warm anyone, but I can burn
With my heart as well as with my tongue.
Which I don't wash or scrub with Brillo.
But whatever I cook up I eat.
Often I was scorched and left unhealed.
Still, I'm no fish on dry land,
Although on dry land I fish for men
With the corner of my eye, the length of my skirt,
Carp fattened with lust
Ready to be caught.
I don't deny it. That's what I do.
I don't give a hoot for all the gossip
Entwined around my name
Like swamp thistle around the reeds.
The sky is above me, that's where I look,
At the stars which I cannot gather.
Nor do I want to.
Let them multiply.
Let them couple and breed.
Let it be like that.

SORRY, GOSPODE

Švorc sam, Gospode.
Prazno srce, prazna pica,
Izvrnuti džepovi moje duše.
U glavi tek ponešto zveči
Kao u konzervi prilog za Crveni krst.
Tutni nešto, Bogo, u moj buđelar.

Prazna sam i bez prebijene,
Srce mi pišti ko čajnik.
Negde vidici pucaju od lepote,
Ovde sumrak pritisko kapke.

Sve sam protraćila, proćerdala.
Sve spiskala.
Sad Ti udeli, nahrani, isceli!
Pre nego što ubeležiš,
Daj pljugu, daj kintu,
Daj kitu, ovoj grešnici.

Daj mi danas.

Niti sijem, niti žanjem,
Niti predem,
Tebe poslušah Bogo,
Sad Ti pobrini se za me.
Izležavam se do podne.
Danju unaokolo cunjam, gluvarim,
Noću nad rukopisima il po barovima
Dreždim, krvarim.
Ujutru stajem na hladan pod srca
Tvog sina, tvog čeda.
Njušim njegovo međunožje
Kao keruša svoje male.

SORRY, MY LORD

I'm penniless, my Lord.
Empty heart, empty pussy.
The pockets of my soul are turned inside out.
In my head something tinkles
As in a Red Cross box.
Slip something in my wallet, Lord.

I'm empty and broke.
My heart whistles like a teakettle.
Elsewhere, landscapes burst with beauty.
Here darkness presses on the eyelids.

I squandered everything, blew it away
As if there was no tomorrow.
Now it's Your turn to give me something.
Feed me, heal me
Before You write it down in Your book.
Give me a butt, a lousy nickel.
Give this sinner a cock.

Give me this day.

I neither sow nor reap,
Nor do I weave.
I obeyed Thee, Lord,
Now You take care of me.
I laze in bed past noon,
Loaf around all day with nothing to do.
Nights I spend in bars or over my manuscripts,
Keep vigil, bleed.
In the morning I step on the cold floor of my heart.
Your son, Your darling,
I sniff between his legs

Jer, Ti kaza:
Sve što hoćete da vama čine ljudi,
Činite i vi tako njima.
Al šutnu me, taj čova,
Istrese me kao pesak iz sandale.
Na podijumu njegovog srca,
Sada plešu druge potpetice,
A moje je prazno i šuplje kao oluk
Kroz koje dobuju ubilačke kapi kiše.

Više mi ništa ne ide od ruke—
Uska vrata, tesan put.
Ne bulji u mene, Bogo,
Ne drži me zemljina teža,
Nacvrcana sam, gubim korak,
Ulica mi je sve krivlja,
Kuća sve dalja,
Pruži ruku, pruži prst,
Ko luču, ne ko prut.
Život cvili kao usna harmonika,
Daleko sam zabasala.
Ne razlikujem više vrste ptica,
Biljaka, drveća, strane sveta,
Rečne od morskih riba,
Izvor od ušća.
Snove po kojima gacam
Od ulice kojom njišem kukovima.

Više puta voleh zauvek,
Moje srce beše vrela ringla,
Sad je vrč razbijen.
Seks neuprljan ljubavlju,
Moja je deviza.

The way a bitch sniffs her litter.
You said: *Do unto others*
As you would have done unto you.
But that man gave me a kick,
Shook me like sand out of a sandal.
I suspect other heels dance now
On his heart's stage
While mine lies hollow like a gutter
Beaten by lethal drops of rain.

Nothing comes easy to me anymore—
Narrow gate, narrow path.
Stop staring at me, Lord.
Gravity won't hold me up.
I'm tipsy, I've lost my footing.
The street grows even more crooked.
My house is even more distant.
Give me Your hand, extend Your finger
Like a torch, not a whip.
Life wails like a mouth organ.
I've thoroughly lost my way.
I can't tell from the birds,
Plants, trees, cardinal points,
Sweetwater fish from the deep-sea kind,
The source from the mouth of a river,
The dreams over which I wade
From the street where I swing my hips.

Many times I fell in love forever.
My heart was a hot stove.
Now the jug is broken.
Let there be sex unstained by love
Is my slogan now.

Sve druge želje stresoh
Kao kišne kapi sa kaputa.
Gospodi pomiluj.
Pevam o duši utopljenoj,
Koju ne mogu na obalu izvući.
Kao obešena divljač vise moje ruke.
Pomozi! Izbavi!
Daj mi—usta na usta!

Voleh gorka pića, žestoke momke,
I koješta još,
Priznajem Ti Bogo,
Ne mimoiđe me nijedan greh.
Kao Tvoje telo,
Moje srce je jastučić za igle.

Sorry, Gospode,
Nisam ja ni Marta ni Marija Magdalena.
Tvoj sam ispljuvak, tvoja slina.
Sad, sve stavi na kantar.
Ne priteži i ne zakidaj.
Odreži!
Obnevidi mi srce, liši me vida.
Patiti i platiti.
Gospodi pomiluj.

Every other desire I shook off
Like raindrops from a coat.
Have mercy, Lord.
I sing of a drowned soul
Which I can't drag to the shore.
My hands hang like wild game.
Help me! Rescue me!
Give me—mouth-to-mouth!

I loved strong drink, violent men,
And other such foolish things.
I confess to You, Lord,
Not a single sin eluded me.
Like Your own body
My heart is a pincushion.

Sorry, Lord.
I'm neither Martha nor Magdalena.
I'm what You spat out, Your discharge.
Now weigh it all on Your scales.
Don't tip them, don't cheat on me.
Go and weigh them.
Blind my heart, take away my sight
To suffer and pay.
Lord, have mercy on me.

JUTARNJI BLUZ

Sama ležem u krevet, sama se budim.
Krmelje brišem, dižem šiju.
Gledam u pod, buljim u tavanicu.
Dići se ili se ponovo stropoštati,
Navući ćebe na glavu ili uposliti tabane?

Svakog jutra isto pitanje, ista potreba,
Urasla u mene kao nokat,
Da mi se prošlost kao iznošena suknja
Ne vuče za petama od sabajle,
Da me svetlost ne ranjava
Svojim puščanim cevima.

Izvući se ispod ćebeta nije sve,
Ne dižem se samo da bih noge protegla.
Da ustanem treba mi bolji razlog,
Od šetanja šešira, kuvanja ručka,
Ili brčkanja Ega u peni i pari lakih komada.

Dojadilo mi je da ležim ovde
Kao zaboravljen prtljag.
Žuljaju me uspomene, budućnost me svrbi,
Kao kopriva žare me svakojake misli.
Za susret sa javom moram biti spremna,
Podesiti nabor na suknji, izraz lica—
Što mi je dojadilo takođe.

Dojadilo mi je da furam sreću,
Da glumatam zadovoljstvo;
Kao da mi je sve potaman,
Kao da mi je baš sad krenulo,
Da sam upravo odigrala životnu rolu
I izvukla na lutriji glavnu premiju.

MORNING BLUES

I go to bed alone and wake alone,
I rub my eyes, stretch my neck,
Look at the floor, stare at the ceiling.
Should I get up or collapse again,
Pull the blanket over my head or busy my feet?

Every morning the same question, the same need
Ingrown like a toenail,
So the past doesn't drag after my heels
First thing in the morning like a worn-out skirt,
So the light doesn't wound me
With a blast from a double-barrel shotgun.

To get from under the covers is not everything.
I don't rise just to stretch my legs.
I need a better reason to get up
Than to promenade my hat, cook my lunch,
Splash my ego in froth and steam of light comedy.

I'm tired of just lying here
Like a forgotten piece of luggage.
Memories pinch me, the future gives me an itch,
Like nettles all kinds of thoughts sting me.
I must prepare myself to meet the day,
Adjust a crease on my skirt, the expression on my face
Everything I've grown weary of.

I'm fed up with faking happiness,
Playacting contentment
As if it was all just fine,
As if things are beginning to go well
Now that I've played the role of my life
And won the big prize at the lottery.

Žudim za nečim čemu ne znam ime.
Za nečim što bi mi izmenilo život
Okrenulo ga tumbe, naglavačke.
Iskliznulo me iz šina,
Kojima se vozim po tačnom redu vožnje.

Došlo mi je da pokupim svoje prnje
I da nekuda zbrišem.
Tamo gde niko ne bi znao za mene.
I gde bih zaboravila na samu sebe,
Kao na ljubavnika sa izbledelim licem.
Da činim samo ono što mi je volja,
Što mi se prohte.

Da za to ne tražm razloge, ne tražim pokriće.
Da jezdim drumovima brzim kolima,
Ne misleći ni na šta i ni na koga,
Dok unaokolo vrućina se tetura,
I klimakterično sunce me prati kao pas lutalica.

I yearn for something I have no name for,
For something that would change my life,
Turn it upside down,
Make it leave the rails on which I travel
Making punctual stops.

I feel like gathering my rags
And making my getaway
Someplace where no one knows about me,
Where I forget about myself
And the pale face of my lover,
To do what I want,
What I damn well please.

I don't need reasons, excuses
To speed down a highway in a fast car
Not thinking about anything or anyone
While around me the heat staggers
And the climacteric sun trails after me like a stray dog.

OBROK

Ne krčkaš više u meni kao u pretis-loncu,
Iskočio je sigurnosni ventil,
Razleteli se po meni tvoji parčići
Kuvani s lovorom, lukom,
I ostalim gorko-slatkim mirođijama,
Koje smo uzajamno dodavali.
Sada te tako raskomadanog
Stavljam na led.
Da te sačuvam za buduće dane
Kada mi ponestane sveže hrane.
Kada u tanjiru ne budem imala
Ništa od zeleniša,
Nijednog od momčića,
Koji se lako vari.
Tada ću u zamrzivač zaviriti,
Izvaditi te, odmrznuti,
I podgrejati—na laganoj vatri.
Dok ne zamirišeš na toplo i poznato.
Na ono od čega ne boli glava.
Samo ponekad naiđe mučnina
Kao od jela više puta podgrevanih
I kusanih dan za danom.
Ali i za to ima leka
Mogla bih te ponuditi nekome
Ko ima dobar stomak ili ko ne bira jela.
Ili ću te izbaciti pred vrata,
Neka te pokusa ona vrtirepka-kuja
Što se ovuda oko kuće mota već neko vreme.

THE MEAL

You no longer hiss in my pressure cooker.
The safety valve blew out.
Your pieces scattered inside me
Cooked with bay leaf, onions,
And other bittersweet herbs
Which we kept adding together.
Dismembered as you are,
I'm putting you on ice
To preserve you for some other day
When I have no fresh food,
No greens on my plate,
Some young boy so easy to digest.
I'll peek into a freezer then,
Take you out and defrost you
And then heat you up over low fire
Until you start giving off
Your warm, familiar smell
That gives no headache,
Only that heavy feeling leftovers give
After being heated too many times
And eaten day after day.
But there's a cure for that too,
I could offer you to someone else
Who has a tough stomach and is not picky.
At long last, I'll set you outside my door.
Let that ass-wiggling bitch sample you,
The one who's been hanging around
My house for some time.

ZIMSKI RUKOPIS

Snežni vrhovi planina,
Beli krinovi,
Jedra vinuta u nebo.
I nebo ustalasano kao stado.

Sve u belo okrečeno.
Prekriveno belim platnom.
Sneg i druge beline
Mislima obojene.

Nema crne šume, crnih ljudi.
Sve žudi za svim.
Stvari kojih se sećaš,
Stvari koje zaboravljaš.
Negde i svuda. Tu.

U tuđini i kod kuće.
Podložno bolu
I stremeći sreći.
Rane noseći svoje,
Prepoznajući užitke,
Telo pamti odsutnog.

Duša se kao i trava
Priseća otiska stopala,
Čari pašnjaka.
Sebe same, žeženog aorista.

O, seti me se ovde,
Gde ljubav se nije pisala,
Nije kušala.

Da niko ne bude nevoljen,
Niko ljubavi pošteđen.

WINTER MANUSCRIPT

The snowy mountain peaks,
White lilies,
Sails raised into the sky
And the sky heaving like a herd.

Everything painted white,
Covered with white canvas.
Snow and that other whiteness
Tinted by thoughts.

There's no black forest, black men.
Everything yearns for everything else.
Things you remember,
Things you forget.
Somewhere and everywhere. Right here.

In a foreign country and at home.
Subject to pain
And aspiring to happiness.
Carrying its wounds,
Recognizing its delights,
The body remembers the absent one.

The soul like the grass
Recalls the foot,
The pleasure of meadows,
Recalls herself alone, the passionate indeterminate.

Oh, remember me here,
Where love was not written down,
Nor sampled,

So no one shall be loveless,
No one shall be spared by love.

BRAČNA POSTELJA

Moj se bok uz tvoj ne primiče više.
Niti tvoja krma uranja u moje morske dubine.
Pod mojim okom ti si pokvašena šibica,
Ja sam paketić smrzlog mesa u frizu tvojih grudi.

To je dovoljno i preko mere,
Da se ne srećemo više pod ovim krovom,
Da se ne mimoilazimo kao na pešačkom prelazu,
Jer nismo ni sustanari ni rođaci,
Različite su nam krvne grupe duše.

Moje grudi nisu biro za izgubljene stvari,
Da bih te tu držala, čuvala,
Dok te neko ne pronađe,
Raspakuje, složi, po svojoj meri
Kao što ja nekad učinih.

Postelja ova nije raka da ležimo u njoj kao mrci.
Nismo ti i ja Romeo i Julija
Da bih nad našim lešom sada lila suze,
A i oplakivanja živih mi je preko glave.

Neću više da naklapam, da se cenjkam
Na temu: voliš—ne voliš.
Moje je srce analfabetsko,
Neću da ga opismenjavam
Za šah-mat, za uzimala-davala.

Ove grudi nisu biro za izgubljene stvari,
Da bih te tu držala, čuvala,
Dok te neko ne pronađe,
Raspakuje, složi, po svojoj meri
Kao što ja nekad učinih.

CONJUGAL BED

My hip doesn't draw close to yours
Nor does your rudder seek my sea depths.
In my eyes you're a wet matchstick.
I'm a package of meat in the freezer of your chest.

That is enough and more than enough.
Let us no longer meet under this roof,
Let us not avoid each other like pedestrians at street crossing
Since we are neither neighbors nor relatives.
The blood type of our souls is different.

These breasts are not a lost-and-found office
For me to keep you and guard you
Till someone doesn't come and find you,
Unwraps you and assembles you as they wish,
The way I myself once did.

This bed is not a grave for us to lie in.
Neither are we Romeo and Juliet
For tears to be shed over our corpses,
And giving a wake for the living is intolerable.

I don't want to prattle and haggle anymore
On the subject of you-love-me-you-don't-love-me.
My heart is an illiterate,
I don't want to teach it how to read
The chessboard of give-and-take.

These breasts are not a lost-and-found department
For me to keep you and guard you
Till someone comes and finds you,
Unwraps you and assembles you as they wish,
The way I myself once did.

Svaka prava cura zna šta joj treba,
Neko ko će joj gristi usne umesto srca,
Ko će joj paliti maštu pod nožnim prstima.

Takvog hoću, takav mi treba.
Za volan sedam i dajem gas.
Ni tebi ne preporučujem rikverc.
Bolji recept nemam.

Every real girl knows what she needs,
Someone to bite her lips and not her heart
And set her imagination on fire under her toes.

That's the kind I want, that's what I need.
I sit behind the wheel and press the gas.
Even to you I don't recommend shifting into reverse.
I can't think of a better recipe.

BLAŽENSTVO ODLASKA

Otperjala sam.
Odsakutala kao veverica.
Čim leto u sandalama dođe,
I ja nazuh svoje.

Popeh se na štikle tanke kao igle
Koje probadaju srce.
Dosta je bilo smrtonosnih rana,
Dosta ratova među državama.
Nagutah se svakojakih pilulica,
Crne tuberoze nicale su odasvuda.

Neću više da sam ičija ruža u reveru,
A ni pojas za spasavanje.
Neću da sam rupa na nečijoj cipeli
Ni cipela koja žulja.

Dok olovku režem, šiljim,
Ne treba mi neko da kraj mene dreždi
Čekajući da na njega pogled bacim
Kao oglodanu kosku gladnom psetu.
Ne treba mi niko da kraj mene hrče
Kao hor testera u šumi
Dok tavanicu pogledom svu noć dubim.

Kao kora hleba dojenčetu
Moji sati potrebni su meni,
Da draškam desni za zube koji će nići,
I kojima ću gristi ono što grizlo je mene.

Samoću svoju neću više ni sa kim da delim.
Upoznah blaženstvo odlaska.

THE BLISS OF DEPARTURE

I flew the coop.
Hopped away like a squirrel.
When summer came in its sandals,
I put on mine.

I stood on heels as thin as needles
That pierce the heart.
There had been enough deadly wounds,
Enough wars between countries.
I swallowed all kinds of tiny pills.
Black warts grew everywhere on me.

I no longer want to be a rose in someone's lapel,
Someone's life jacket,
A hole in someone's shoe,
Nor the shoe that pinches.

I sharpen the pencil to a point.
I don't need anyone to sit next to me
Waiting for me to throw him a glance
Like a gnawed bone to a hungry dog.
I don't want anyone to snore next to me
Like a choir of saws in a forest
While I drill the ceiling with my eyes all night long.

Like a crust of bread to an infant
I need my hours for myself
To rub the gums where teeth will grow
With which to bite what once bit me.

I won't share my solitude with anyone.
I came to know the bliss of departure.

Sada sve svoje vreme držim u šaci,
Niko mi ga ne može komadati.

Il se prelistavam il zatvaram korice,
Il se izležavam il upošljavam tabane.
Pa put pod noge daleko od Jave,
Srećicu da pecam na dokovima Mašte!

Now I hold my time in the palm of my hand.
No one can break it into pieces.

I either thumb the pages or close the covers,
Or lie around and keep my feet occupied.
So, let's go far from reality and fish for happiness
On the piers of the imagination!

TWO

LIRSKE POSLEDICE

Bez metafora, moj gospodičiću!
Da, imam podvaljak,
Imam podočnjake,
Imam sede.
Sredovečna žena,
A Vi—junoša!

Da, podnapita sam i bleda.
I žica mi na čarapi gmiže
Uz nogu kao zmija.
Da, hendikepirana sam.
Zakopčanog grla.
Srce mi je ledeni breg,
Ne pomišljajte da ga otopite.

Jeste, spržena sam pustinja,
Hananski mrka.
Nisam Vaša mala hrizantema
O koju bi da stidnik češete.

Jest' osorna sam.
Jest' divlja sam.
Raspusna.
Katkad u purpur obučena.
Laso bacam ždrepcima oko vrata.
Usnice im svoje pružam-čedne.
Al od Vas u stranu ih okrećem.

O, tako jednostavan čin—
Kao kada noć pada po svemu!

LYRIC CONSEQUENCES

Without metaphors, my dear Sir!
Yes, I have a double chin,
Circles under my eyes.
I have gray hairs.
I'm a middle-aged woman.
And you, young buck!

Yes, I'm tipsy and pale.
The run in my stocking
Crawls up my leg like a snake.
Yes, I'm handicapped
With a buttoned-up throat.
My heart is an iceberg,
Don't imagine you can thaw it.

Yes, I'm a scorched desert,
Dark-skinned as a Bedouin.
I'm no longer the little chrysanthemum
For you to scratch your balls with.

Yes, I'm harsh.
Yes, I'm wild.
Immoral woman.
At times dressed in purple.
I lasso the colts,
Offer them my virginal lips
While turning them away from you.

Oh, what a simple act—
As when night falls on one and all!

MA SOEUR

On hrče, *ma soeur.*
Ja kraj njega ležim,
Gledam u nebo boginjavo od zvezda,
U adolescentni mesec što lagano plovi,
Kao čun morem posle bure.

Sve je mirno,
Samo u meni tako nije.
Dva smo ostrva u istom arhipelagu,
Na jednom je umor žege,
Na drugom kosti se lede, *ma soeur.*
On me ispi kao flašu piva
A moja ljubav se istopi
Kao kocka šećera u ustima, tako bi.

Sada noćima ovako ležim.
Slušam kišu kako dobuje po mom srcu.
Nekada vetar mrsi grane,
A nekada, kao sad što je,
Namotavam mesečinu na prste
I otapam uspomene kao smrzlo povrće.
Za to nije potrebno dvoje,
Zar ne, *ma soeur?*

Pijem crnu tintu.
Crnu tintu za crne dane, *ma soeur.*
Mucam pomrčinu,
Dok napolju mesec sipi srebro na grane
Sa kojih opadaju moje prezrele žudnje.

Još samo kada bih mogla
Od očaja nutrinu da pometem, *ma soeur,*

MA SOEUR

He's snoring, *ma soeur.*
I lie next to him,
Stare into the sky pockmarked with stars,
The adolescent moon that slowly floats
Like a rowboat after a storm.

All is quiet
Except inside me.
We are two islands in the same archipelago,
On one, there's heat and exhaustion,
And on the other, bones freeze, *ma soeur.*
He drank me like a bottle of beer.
My love melted like a sugar cube
In the mouth. That's the way it was.

Many nights I lie like this,
Listening to the rain beat on my heart.
At times the wind entangles the branches.
At times, like now,
I wind the moonlight on my fingers,
Thaw memories like frozen vegetables.
For that, don't you agree, *ma soeur,*
One doesn't need two people?

I drink black ink,
Black dye for black days, *ma soeur.*
I stutter darkness while outdoors
The moon drips silver on the branches
From which my overripe longings fall.

If only I had the capacity
To scramble my innards out of anguish, *ma soeur.*

I da zapevušim nešto
O zvezdama koje dogorevaju,
Ili Suncu što izranja iz modre noći
Kao iz morskih talasa mlad Bog—
Moja posestrimo po mastilu, ili čežnji.

To start singing about stars
That are burning out,
Or the sun rising out of the purple night
Like a young god out of sea waves.
Oh, my sister in ink and yearning.

O, BITI SAMA

O, biti sama
Bez tvoga hoda, tvoga glasa.
O, tišinu čuti poput rasta
Tamnog cveta u kutku sobe.
O biti usred ćutanja stvari i uma.
O, biti sama
Bez tvoga hoda, tvoga glasa.
O, čuti samo kucanje svoga srca,
Tihovati kao pečurka usred vlažne šume.
O, pružiti se preko kreveta
Kao slomljena grana.
O, priljubljena biti uz tišinu
Kao list uz mokri asfalt.
O, biti sama
Bez tvog hoda, tvog glasa, tvoga tela,
Tišinom pokrivena, obmotana.
O, čuti noć kako se zgušnjava.
O, ležati sama, budna,
Dok mesečev zrak pada na krevet
Kao hladan mač.
O, čuti tišinu poput sovinog krika.
O, biti bez tvoga glasa, tvoga tela,
Kao u grob položena.

OH, TO BE ALONE

Oh, to be alone
Without your footsteps, your voice.
Oh, to hear the silence like the growing
Of a dark flower in a corner of a room.
Oh, to be in the quiet of things and the quiet mind.
Oh, to be alone
Without your footsteps, your voice.
Oh, to hear only the beating of your heart,
Keeping quiet like a mushroom in a damp forest.
Oh, to stretch across the bed
Like a broken branch.
Oh, to snuggle up to the silence
Like a leaf to the wet pavement.
Oh, to be alone
Without your footsteps, voice and your body,
Covered with silence, wrapped in it.
Oh, to hear the night thicken.
Oh, to lie alone wide awake
While a ray of moonlight falls on the bed
Like a cold sword.
Oh, to hear the silence like a shriek of the owl.
Oh, to be without your voice, your body
As if laid out in a tomb.

NIJE NIKAKVA

Pogledaj je, nije nikakva.
Oči su joj kao zrna bibera.
Zubi su joj kao u veverice,
Usta prevrnuta čarapa.
Toroče bez prestanka,
Brunda kao medved,
Krekeće kao žaba.

Za razliku od mene.

Pogledaj je, nije nikakva.
Noge su joj kao dorski stubovi,
Ruke su joj bokserske.
Ide kao pokretna bačva,
Valja se kao bure,
Ne možeš je obujmiti,
Debela je kao klada.

Za razliku od mene.

Pogledaj je, nije nikakva.
Oblači se kao popadija,
Suknjama mete zemlju,
Na njima je kilo blata,
Ispod...
Sigurno nije ništa bolje.

Za razliku od mene

SHE'S NOTHING TO LOOK AT

Look at her; she's nothing to look at.
Her eyes are peppercorns.
She has the teeth of a squirrel.
Her mouth is a sock turned inside out.
She talks all the time.
Grumbles like a bear.
Croaks like a frog.

Unlike me.

Look at her; she's nothing to look at.
Her legs are like Doric columns,
Her hands are that of a boxer.
She walks like a moving tub,
Rolls like a barrel.
You can't put your hands around her.
She's as fat as a tree log.

Unlike me.

Look at her; she's nothing to look at.
She dresses like a minister's wife.
Her skirts sweep the ground.
There must be a pound of mud on them,
Underneath…
Surely, it's not much better.

Unlike me.

Pogledaj je,
Stoji kao kečer,
Koji je upravo odneo pobedu
Na važnom takmičenju.

Za razliku od mene.

Look at her,
She stands like a professional wrestler
Who has just won a victory
At a championship match.

Unlike me.

NEDELJA

Nedeljom obično dugo krmeljam.
Baškarim se u krevetu, brčkam u kadi.
Vučem se po kući po ceo dan u pidžami.
Niti koga primam, niti gde izlazim.

Ne dumam mnogo.
Ne pokušavam da zaboravim,
Ne pokušavam da se setim.
Gledam sebi da ugodim.
Čim mi se misao uhvati za neku kvaku
Ja skrstim ruke il zapalim cigaru.
Dimom teram demone u kratkim pantalonama,
Što se unaokolo šunjaju i prikradaju.

Sa mnom u kući sve je u dremežu.
Pospano, lenjo kao i ja:
Sto i stolice, tepisi po kojima gazim,
Saksije sa cvećem i cveće u vazi,
Knjige i njihovi junaci—
Svi polegali kao na ladanju.

Dobro se slažemo,
Ničije nam društvo ne fali.
Oni dremaju
A ja se ugnezdim u stih
Kao vrabac pod strehu.

SUNDAY

Sundays I usually shilly-shally,
Idle in bed, splash in the tub.
I drag myself around the house in pajamas.
I receive no one, do not go out.

I don't do much thinking,
Make no effort to forget,
Make no effort to remember.
I pamper myself,
So the moment some thought
Gets caught by a door handle,
I cross my arms, light a cigarette
And with its smoke chase away demons in short pants
That lurk around me and draw close.

Everything in my house drowses,
Everything is sleepy and lazy like me.
Table and chairs, the carpets over which I walk,
Flower pots and flowers in a vase,
The books and their heroes—
Are all napping as if they were vacationing.

We all get along just fine.
We don't need anybody.
They doze
While I make myself a nest in some verse
Like a sparrow under the eaves.

JA SAM STAROMODNA CURA

Ja sam stromodna cura,
Volim kuće prizemljuše krastavih zidova
Sa dvorištima krcatim starudijama,
Umesto oblakodera i apartmana
U kojima se budim i spavam.
Muškatle u prozorima i u loncima na tufne
Više volim od imitacija, od «veštaka».
Ja sam staromodna cura,
Što više voli vespe umesto automobila.
Tamndrkanje tramvaja i kloparanje parnjače,
Više od zvižduka mlaznjaka,
Puteljke umesto avenija i bulevara,
Kojima moje potpetice odzvanjaju.
Ja sam staromodna cura,
Što voli miris opranog veša
Koga vetar naduvava
Do moga lica, preko moga nosa,
I sve ono što veje iz prethodnog života.
Ja sam staromodna cura,
Još slušam longplejke i tipkam na *Olivetti*.
Govorim hvala, izvinite, molim.
Volim da mi dasa pripali cigaretu,
Otvori vrata, pridrži kaput, primakne stolicu,
Da me svlači krpicu po krpicu.
Ja sam staromodna cura,
Što voli kič scene sa zalascima sunca,
Modne žurnale i porodične albume,
Od okretnih igara «stiskavac» jedino razumem.
Nove filmove još gledam na stari način,
Iz zadnjeg reda bioskopske polutame,
Vežbajući «francuski poljubac».
Ja sam staromodna cura,
Ne zujim i ne skitaram kojekuda,

I'M AN OLD-FASHIONED GIRL

I'm an old-fashioned girl.
I like low houses with pockmarked walls
With yards full of junk
Instead of skyscrapers and apartment houses
Where I wake and sleep.
Geraniums on windowsills in polka-dot cans
I prefer to artificial flowers.
I'm an old-fashioned girl,
That likes a scooter better than an automobile,
The rattle of a streetcar,
The rumble of a steam locomotive,
More than a whistle of a jet plane.
Footpaths instead of avenues and boulevards
Where my heels go clicking.
I'm an old-fashioned girl,
That likes the smell of clean laundry
The wind brings to my face, over my nose,
Everything that falls like snow in my previous life.
I'm an old-fashioned girl,
I still listen to long-playing records
And type on an Olivetti.
I say thank you, please, excuse me.
I like when a gentleman gives me a light,
Opens the door for me,
Holds my coat, offers me a chair,
And takes my clothes off garment by garment.
I'm an old-fashioned girl,
That likes kitschy landscapes with sunsets,
Fashion magazines and family albums.
Close dancing is the only kind I understand.
I watch the new movies in the old way
Sitting in the half-dark,
Practicing French-kissing in the last row.

U kući dreždim povazdan,
Kao glineni ćup sušeći se na promaji
Samoće i zadovoljstava,
Mamurna od snova.
Ja sam staromodna cura
Što se kuva u sopstvenom loncu
Marke hoću-neću.
O ljubavi i strasti malo šta znam,
Devičijeg srca rođena udovica,
Pod čijim nogama život kulja
Kao para iz šahta
Koju zaobilazim brzim koracima.
Ja sam staromodna cura,
Ne kupujem po sniženoj ceni
Ni osmehe ni svilu.
Ne nosim mini suknje i dekoltee,
Bilo bi to lako oružje za nekog
Ko je nameran da osvaja bez.
Ja sam staromodna cura
Niti psujem, niti zvocam, niti besnim,
Možete me mazati na hleb.
Al s medom se uvek dobije malo otrova,
Ljubavi u smrtonosnim dozama.
Ja sam staromodna cura,
Stari momak žulja me kao nova cipela,
Koju moram izuti, zameniti.
Za jednog udobnog kao patika,
Ili razgaženog kao susetkin muž.
Ja sam staromodna cura,
Dobra prema muškarcima,
Kao prema onima koji se plaše mraka,
Lifta i prelaska ulice van pešačkog prelaza.
Ja sam staromodna cura,

I'm an old-fashioned girl,
I don't go buzzing around,
I'm always to be found at home
Like a clay pot drying in the draft
Of solitude and contentment,
Hungover from all the dreaming.
I'm an old-fashioned girl,
That's cooking her own casserole
Called I-want-I-don't-want.
I know little about love and passion,
A widow born with a virgin's heart
Under whose feet life pours out
Like steam out of a manhole
Which I avoid with my quick steps.
I'm an old-fashioned girl,
I buy nothing at bargain rates,
Neither smiles nor rolls of silk.
I don't wear miniskirts and low-cut dresses
To make it easy for whoever
Wants to steal a kiss.
I'm an old-fashioned girl,
I don't cuss, complain or rage.
You can spread me on your toast,
Although honey always comes with a bit of poison,
Love in fatal doses.
I'm an old-fashioned girl,
My old boyfriend pinches me like a new shoe
Which I need to take off, replace
With someone as comfortable as a slipper
Or broken in like my neighbor's husband.
I'm an old-fashioned girl,
Nice to all the guys
As I am to all those who are afraid of the dark,

Drevna kao Kartagina,
Minimalno oštećena zubom vremena.
Muzejski komad koga nema na aukciji.
Pipanje nije dozvoljeno.
Uzmi ili ostavi!

Afraid of elevators
And crossing the street where it's not allowed.
I'm an old-fashioned girl,
As ancient as Carthage,
Minimally damaged by the tooth of time.
A museum piece that is not at auction.
Touching is not permitted.
Take it or leave it!

METAFIZIKA SUMRAKA

Prekasno je da ičemu učim srce,
Naizust znam azbuku patnje—
Proveravam uživo.
Život zna više od Sibile.

Vreme je stalo.
Kakvo blaženstvo je u proticanju?
Stvarnost podseća na umoljičan đžemper—
Ovo su stihovi.
Život ipak šepa, poput kakve uboge devojke
Koja bi da se dobro uda
Iako u srcu nosi ožiljke uspomena—
Životopis vatre i vode.
To su te zaludne i bolne zalihe
Sa kojima se polazi na dug i neizvestan put
Koji je naša lična otadžbina,
Na koju svačija noga stupa kao čizma.

Od Kaina starija je svaka patnja,
Pa i ova koja je kao rođaka iz daleka
Došla na tri dana, a ostala,
Raskomotila se, zauzela svaki kutak.
O odlasku ni da bekne!

Vreme čuda je za nama.
Vreme građenja kula,
Rajskih i ovozemaljskih vrtova
Iz čitanki i stihova.
Tzv. grčka sreća čeka nas
Tamo gde nikada nećemo stiči.
Zato napoj cveće i srce
Iz istog krčaga, ako ikako možeš.
Vreme ne presahnjuje,

TWILIGHT METAPHYSICS

It's too late to teach my heart anything.
The alphabet of suffering
I already know it by heart. I test it live.
Life knows more than the Sibyl.

Time has stopped. What bliss is there in flowing?
Reality resembles a moth-eaten sweater—
This is what poetry is like.
Life limps like a crippled girl
Who hopes to marry well
Even though her heart is scarred with memories.
Biography of fire and water.
These are the worthless and painful reserves
With which one starts on a long, uncertain journey
Over one's own private homeland
On which everyone steps on in boots.

Every suffering is older than Cain,
Even this one which like a cousin from far away
Has come for a three-day visit
And stayed, made herself comfortable,
Took up all the room—
And said nothing about leaving!

The time of miracles is behind us.
Time of tower-building,
Heavenly and earthly gardens
From schoolbooks and poems.
The so-called Greek luck awaits us
Where we will never arrive.
Therefore, if you can,
Water the flowers and the heart
From the same pitcher.
Time doesn't dry up,

Niti ubrzava korak, kako vele.
Vreme guta sopstvene slike kao sopstvenu decu.

Znaj, neće ti pomoći
Nikakvo navlačenje jorgana na glavu,
Makar te pod njim čekalo drago telo.
Nikakvo stavljanje voska u uši.
Sirenina pesma biće deo tvog urlika.

Rođeni srećni i manje srećni
Umiru pre smrti svojih tela,
Vlastito lice noseći kao tuđu odeću,
Poput likova sa slika Hijeronimusa Boša.

Onaj ko je napisao nebo, zemlju, more,
A naročito ko je napisao sneg i snove,
Mesečeve mene, boje lišća, naša lica
Dalek se čini i hladan kao severni pol.

Ne zovi to nihilizmom ni bogohuljenjem.
Pogrešna sintaksa, loša dikcija
Beše stvaranje sveta—
Toliko je jabuka razdora bačeno među nas,
Da će se jedna dokotrljati i do tvojih nogu.
Možda baš onda kada budeš skupio letinu,
Sveo račune.
Kada budeš zabacio ruke iznad glave
Terajući u vis kolutove dima i sanje.

Mrtvorođene biće tvoje želje.
Udovička svaka nada.
A ljubavi ni koliko da namažeš na krišku hleba.

Nor makes steps quicker, as they say.
Time swallows its own images
As if they were its children.

Get it through your head, throwing a blanket
Over your face won't help you,
Even if underneath it a dear body waits for you.
No use stuffing wax in your ears either.
The siren's song will be a part of your scream.

Those born happy and less happy
Die before their own body dies.
They wear their faces like other people's clothes
As in paintings by Hieronymus Bosch.

The one who wrote the sky, the earth and the sea,
And above it all, snow and dreams,
The phases of the moon, the color of leaves, our faces,
Seems distant and cold like the North Pole.

Don't call that nihilism or blasphemy.
The world was created
With wrong syntax and bad diction—
So many apples of divisiveness
Have been tossed between us,
One of them will roll even at your feet,
Perhaps, just as you've brought in the harvest,
Added up the accounts,
Thrown your hands over your head
Chasing rings of smoke and reveries.

Your wishes will be dead at birth.
Your every hope will be a widow.
And as for love, there won't be enough
To spread on a slice of bread.

ŽENSKO PISMO

Neću da budem poslušna i krotka.
Mazna kao mačka. Privržena kao pseto.
Sa stomakom do zuba, sa rukama u testu,
Sa licem od brašna, sa srcem-ugljenom,
I njegovom rukom na mojoj zadnjici.

Neću da budem zastavica-dobrodošlica
Na njegovom kućnom pragu.
Ni zmija čuvarkuća pod tim pragom.
Ni zmija, ni Eva, iz priče o Postanju.

Neću da hodam između vrata i prozora,
Da osluškujem i razabiram
Korake od noćnih šumova.
Neću da pratim olovno pomeranje kazaljki
Ni padanje zvezda—
Da bi se on pijan *zaglibio u mene kao slon.*

Neću da budem udenuta goblen bodom
U porodičnu sliku:
Kraj kamina s klupčićima dece,
U vrtu s kučićima dece.
Pa, ja kao hlad-drvo.
Pa, ja kao zimski pejzaž.
Statueta pod snegom
U venčanici s naborima i volanima
Odleteću u nebo.

Aleluja! Aleluja!
Neću mladoženju.

A WOMAN'S LETTER

I don't want to be obedient and tame.
Coddled like a cat. Faithful like a dog.
With a belly up to my teeth, hands in the dough,
Face covered with flour, my heart a cinder
And his hand on my ass.

I don't want to be a welcome flag at his door,
Nor the guardian snake under his threshold,
Neither the snake nor Eve from Genesis.

I don't want to pace between the door and the window,
To listen hard and be able to distinguish
Footsteps from night sounds.
I don't want to follow the leaden movement of the watch hands,
Nor see falling stars
For him to gore me drunkenly like an elephant.

I don't want to be sewn with needlepoint
To the family portrait
Next to the fireplace with balled-up children,
In the garden with little tots,
And I— the shade tree.
And I— the winter landscape,
A statue under the snow.
In a pleated wedding dress
I'll fly to heaven.

Alleluia! Alleluia!
I don't want a bridegroom.

Hoću sedu kosu, hoću grbu ikotaricu,
Pa da krenem u šumu,
Da berem jagode i skupljam suvarke.

Da je već sve za mnom,
I osmeh onog mladića
Tada tako drag i ničim zamenjiv.

I want gray hair, a hump and a basket
To go roaming in the woods,
Picking strawberries and dry twigs.

With my whole life behind me,
The smile of that boy,
Once so dear and completely irreplaceable.

ONA DRUGA

Dok čitam crne hronike,
Među namerno ili slučajno ubijenima,
Među nestalim ili samoubijenima
—tražim tvoje ime.

Dok na TV-u obaveštavaju
O teškim saobraćajnim nesrećama,
O požarima, poplavama i sličnim katastrofama
—zamišljam da si među unesrećenima.

Kad god telefon zazvoni u nevreme,
Kad vidim poštara sa telegramom u ruci,
Kad god čujem: «Tužna vest...»
—pomislim, izovoriće tvoje ime.

U čituljama priviđa mi se tvoj lik.
Na nadgrobnim pločama toliko ti je sličnih.
Na svakoj samrtnoj postelji ležiš ti.
U ogledalu vidim tvoje lice.

Posle toliko smrti, toliko umiranja
—nemoguće je da si živa.
Iako smrt nije zgoditak na lutriji
—kako dobitnik nisi ti?!

Moja mala crna haljina čeka da je obučem,
Nekad je služila za svečane izlaske
—sad vreba ovakve prilike.

Staviću i crni veo ako treba,
I stati uz najbliže ožalošćene.
Najdraža za života—najdraža pokojnica.

THE OTHER ONE

While reading the death notices,
Among the deliberately and accidentally killed,
Among the suicides and the disappeared,
I search for your name.

While they speak on television
Of serious traffic accidents,
Fires, floods and similar catastrophes,
I imagine you among the victims.

Whenever the phone rings at an odd hour,
Whenever I see a mailman with a telegram,
Whenever I hear "sad news,"
I think they'll say your name.

In the obituaries I imagine your face.
On gravestones so many resemble you.
On every deathbed you lie.
In the mirror I see your face.

After so much death, so much dying—
Impossible that you can be still alive.
Even if death is not a lottery,
How is it that you are not the winner?

My small black dress waits to be worn.
At one time it went to parties.
Now it watches for that other occasion.

If need be, I'll wear a black veil,
Stand close to the mourners,
Dearest in life, dearest in death.

Samo da budem obaveštena.
Da saznam na vreme.
Da ne otputujem nekuda.
Da budem na licu mesta;

Kada bude pala poslednja grudva zemlje
Život da uzmem u svoje ruke
I odložim ga na stranu kao dete—

Ja turistkinja u službi večnosti,
Što pod tuđim imenom živi.
Osećam zemlju na kapcima.

May I be the one to hear the news,
Hear it on time,
So I don't go traveling,
So I'm not right here.

When the last lump of earth falls—
To take life into my hand
And push it aside like a child.

I, the tourist in service of eternity,
Living under another's name.
I can feel the dirt on my eyelids.

«ANTROPOMORFNI ORMAR»

Više nema mesta. Prepuni smo kao ormari.
Ono što smo slagali, red po red,
Savijali, pakovali. Previjali na rane.
Ono što smo kačili na kuke,
Ređali na vešalice;
Zimske želje, letnje snove,
Sunčeve zalaske, snežne vrhove,
Tvoje-moje uzdahe-jecaje—
Sad ispremeštano leži ovde-onde.

Zaboravljeno. Skinuto u žurbi.
Bačeno u ćoše. Okrenuto naopačke.
Ono neophodno i ono manje važno
Nabacano jedno preko drugog sad je.
I okraćalo. I tesno. I skrojeno po meri.
I izbledelo, i šljašteće—tu je.

Slomljeno Adamovo rebarce.
Otkinuto anđeosko krilo.
Krzno ljubavi i ljubav s flekom.
Prstenje. Češljevi. Duhovi. Moljci.
Niko se tu više ne može snaći.
Gde se delo? Prevrni! Pomeri!
Izgubljeno. Pa ponovo nađeno.
Odbačeno. Pa u zagrljaj vraćeno.

Leluja paučina. Miš gricka.
Leptir širi krila.
Trn u oku. More na izdisaju.
Dan-noć. Voli-ne voli.
Izbaci-ubaci. Daj-uzmi.
Ovo na hemijsko. Ovo Luciferu.
Ovo Ciganki. A ovo—nikako!

ANTHROPOMORPHIC WARDROBE

There's no more room. We are full.
Everything we stored, layer by layer,
Folded, packed in as if bandaging wounds.
Belongings we hung by a hook,
Belongings we lined up on hangers,
Winter wishes, summer dreams,
Sunsets, snowy peaks,
What's yours-what's mine, sighs and sobs—
Now shifted every which way.

Forgotten. Taken down in a hurry.
Thrown in the corner. Turned inside out.
What is indispensable and what is less so
Thrown on top of one another.
Once made to measure, then grown short,
Grown too tight, faded or shiny—it's all here.

Adam's little broken rib.
The plucked angel's wing.
Venus's fur and love-stain.
Rings. Combs. Ghosts. Moths.
No one can find anything here.
Where is it? Turn it upside down! Rummage!
Lost, then found again.
Rejected, then cherished again.
Cobwebs sway. The mouse gnaws.
The butterfly spreads its wings.

Torn in the eye. The sea on its last breath.
Night-day. Loves-doesn't love.
Throw it-keep it. Give-take.
This to the dry cleaners. This to the devil.
This to the Salvation Army. And this—not in your life!

Nabori žudnje. Isparano srce.
Plačni muslin. Arijadnine niti.
Pridevske čipkice. Aoristi.
Rečenice-restlovi. Krljušti reči.
Iz fioka vire, vise. Obamrli. Večni.
Cure. Kaplju. Liju suze. Liju slasti.
Sline sati. Život iznošeni.

The creases of lust. Washed-out heart.
Weepy muslin. Ariadne's thread.
Adjectival lace. Aorist.
Sentence-rags. Flake of words. Peek out
Of drawers, dangle. Expired. Eternal.
Trickle. Ooze. Shed tears. Drip pleasures.
The snivel of time passing. Used-up life.

ZADOVOLJSTVA

Nekoliko stihova.

Nekoliko redaka o stihovima.

Nekoliko gutljaja

Nečeg gustog i gorkog niz grlo.

Veče što spušta svoje umorno telo.

Sećanje.   Tišina.

Jedva čujno tik-takanje.

Još samo da padne letnji pljusak.

Ležati uz nečiji pupak. Da!

PLEASURES

A few verses.

A few lines about poetry.

A few sips down the throat

Of something thick and bitter.

The evening lowers its weary bones.

Memory.   Silence.

The barely audible tick-tack.

If only there was a summer shower.

My head next to someone's navel. Yes!

DOBROTA

Dobrota je dosadna.
Gospa Dobrota i sva njena dobročinstva!
Dosadno je biti dobar.
Praštati, biti ljubazan.
Smešiti se,
I zadržati smešak.
Dozlaboga dosadno!
Poturati tanjirić mleka
Pod svaku njuškicu.
Obraz,
Poturati pod svačiji dlan.
Pokušala sam to.
Ali nije mi išlo.

Samo: na! na! na!
Bez: daj!
Takvima je mesto na nebu,
Međ svetcima.
A ja nisam ta.
Tek tamo mora da je dosadno!
Neću tamo ni za živu glavu,
Još mi se ovde pravi dar-mar!

Izgleda, za pakao se spremam,
Isuviše često pokazujem zube.
Osetljiva sam, dragi, kao skotna kučka—
U stanju sam da rastrgnem svakog
Ko mi priđe blizu,
Ali i da polopćem sopstveni nakot—
Za spas tela-duše.
Zato nisam oštenila ni jedno.
U utrobi ih svojoj držim, čuvam.
Sa srcem međ zubima,
Na sve režim.

GOODNESS

Goodness is boring.
Mrs. Goodness herself with her charities!
It's boring to be good.
To forgive, be polite,
To smile
And keep smiling.
Dreadfully boring.
Sticking a saucer of milk
Under every snout,
Offering your cheek
To every hand to slap.
I've tried all that,
But I couldn't make it go.

Only: take! take! take!
Never: give!
That kind of woman belongs in heaven
In company of saints.
I'm not the type.
Besides, it must be really boring there!
Not in your life will I go.
I still want to make whoopee down here!

It seems it's hell I'm getting myself ready for.
Too often I bare my teeth.
I'm sensitive, my love, like a pregnant bitch—
Capable of tearing anyone apart
Who comes close to me
Even eating my own pups
For the salvation of body and soul.
That's why I never brought one forth.
I keep them in my womb, guard them
With my heart between my teeth.
I growl at everyone.

JESENJA ODA

Slavicu oktobar a ne maj,
Striptiz stabala umesto prolećnih orgazama.
Predsmrtni čas travke, latice i lista,
Umesto napirlitanih stabala i stabljika,
Nakinđurenih kao udavače na korzou.

Previše je đinđuva, đžiđža-miđža,
Drangulija i ostalih ukrasa. Previše kiča,
Po vratovima grana i ušima peteljaka.
Više mi prija puritanska jesen,
Od proleća što puca od zdravlja
Kao mlad atleta
Sa bicepsima dignutim u nebo.

Od invazije zelenog, od terora boja,
Više mi prija pacifizam ćilibara—
Žuto, mrko, oker.
Anemično nebo draže mi je
Od menstruiranja sunca.

Od erekcije pupoljaka draža mi je
Svaka klonula glava ruže.
A od bludničenja pčele i cveta
Draži mi je list što žuti i kašljuca
Kao bolesnik od TB-a—
S njim usklađujem boju, ritam.
Jer, koliko juče,
Osetih smrtonosni ujed proleća.

AUTUMN ODE

I'll celebrate October and not May,
The striptease of trees instead of orgasm of blossoms,
Grass, petal and leaf at death's door
Instead of well-groomed trees and stalks
Decked out like marriageable girls on a stroll.

Too many gewgaws, trinkets,
Knickknacks and ornaments,
Too much bad taste
On the necks of branches and ears of petals.
The puritan autumn suits me more
Than spring bursting with health
Like a young athlete
With his biceps raised to heaven.

I prefer the pacifism of amber,
Yellow, brown, ocher
To green invasion and terror of color.
The anemic sky is dearer to me
Than the periodic bleeding of the sun.

Every flattened rose
Is dearer to me than the erection of buds
Or the whoring bee and flower.
I like the leaf turning yellow and coughing
Like a TB patient.
I match my color and my rhythm with it
Since just yesterday
I felt the lethal bite of spring.

DOĐI I LEZI PORED MENE

Šta politika, šta berze?!
Dođi i lezi pored mene.
Proklijaću kao krompir u podrumu,
Dok stanu ratovi, revolucije, štrajkovi,
Dok se umnože deonice, dok skoče tantijeme,
Dok se na grani zazelene novčanice.

Dole-gore cent ili groš,
Profit ili bankrot—
Sve su to trice i kučine,
Ako ne legneš pored mene
Biću kao isceđen stih.

Istina i pravda, viši ciljevi,
Strašni Sud i Novi Rim—
Sve su to smislili samo da nas rastave.
Daj, dođi i lezi pored mene,
Da ne skončam kraj nečije čizme
Ili pod njom.

Telo ti dajem na revers,
Dušu na poček.
Od tvoga bitka
Treba mi jedino tvoj mišić-stidnik.
Daj, dođi i lezi pored mene,
Pribij se uz moje srce.
Napolju kao meso od kostiju opada lišće.

COME AND LIE NEXT TO ME

To hell with politics, with the stock market!
Come and lie next to me.
I'll sprout like a potato in the cellar
Till wars, revolutions, strikes all end,
Till shares multiply, bonuses increase,
Till money grows on trees.

The rising or falling value of a cent,
Profit or bankruptcy.
All these are mere trifles.
If you don't lie next to me
I'll be like a line of verse wrung dry.

Truth and justice, the higher pursuits,
Last Judgment and New Rome—
All that they invented
So they can separate us.
Come and lie next to me, please,
So I don't end up next to a boot
Or under it.

I give you my body on credit,
My soul on the layaway plan.
From your innermost being
I need your love muscle only.
Come and lie next to me,
Snuggle up to my heart.
Outside the leaves are falling
Like meat from the bone.

LETNJA PESMA

Moj nije niko i ničija nisam ja.

Šipurak zaseo pod prozor,
Kao momče sa brčićima.

Paprat i kopriva
Ruku pod ruku puteljkom.

Ladolež kao gušter opružen
Na suncu.

Grozd otežao nad kućnom obrvom.
Na stolu lubenica kao srce prepuklo.

Moj nije niko i ničija nisam ja.

SUMMER SONG

I'm nobody's and I have nobody of my own.

Dog rose sits under my window
Like a youth with a mustache.

Fern and nettle arm in arm
Go down a little path.

Bindweed sprawls like a lizard
In the sun.

Grapes grow heavy over the house.
A watermelon cracks like a heart on the table.

I'm nobody's and I have nobody of my own.

THREE

EVERGREEN

Dosta mi je usamljenih žena.
Tužnih. Ucveljenih. Napuštenih.
Čije duše plutaju
Kao boce s porukom bačene u more.
Dosta mi je narikača.
Dosta saučesnica, družbenica, sestara.
Usedelica i udavača. Večnih udovica,
Čija srca cure i kaplju
Poput pokvarenih slavina.
Dosta mi je tog pogrebnog marša.
Nemam više ništa s vama.

Dosta mi je majčica skočica
I vernih ljuba oborenog pogleda—
Čuvarkuća lanjskih snegova i rajskih vrtova.
Dosta mi je vaših spomenara i herbarijuma,
Ispresovanih himena i ispeglanih bora.

Dosta, vaših zamrznutih talenata
Što se krčkaju u loncu Njegovog omiljenog jela.
Vaše crne džigerice i pohovanog mozga.
Vaših praznih kreveta i uglancanog parketa
Po kome klizi mesečina
Umesto *šekspirovske životinje s dvoje leđa.*
Nemam ništa s vama.

Dosta mi je vaših otežalih zadnjica,
Podvaljaka, podočnjaka, pobačaja.
Vaših dijeta, depilacija, ondulacija.
Vaših dekoltea, visokih potpetica,
Šliceva, i ostalih udica.
Dosta mi je te nožice ispod stola,
Tog pogleda ispod oka.

EVERGREEN

I've had enough of lonely women.
Sad. Miserable. Abandoned women
Whose souls float like bottles
Thrown in the sea with a message.
Enough of professional mourners.
Enough of companions, sisters, dispensers of condolences.
Old maids and marrying types,
Eternal widows whose hearts leak and drip
Like rusty faucets.
Enough of that funeral march.
I don't want anything more to do with you.

Enough of Mother Hubbards
And faithful wives with their eyes lowered—
The guardians of last year's snows and Gardens of Eden.
Enough of your herbariums and picture albums,
Dried up beavers and ironed-out wrinkles.

Enough of your frozen talents
Simmering with His favorite dish in a pot.
Your black liver and fried brains.
Your empty beds and waxed floors
Over which moonlight slides
Instead of Shakespeare's beast with two backs.
I have nothing in common with you.

Enough of your big asses,
Double chins, circles under the eyes, abortions,
Diets, depilations, hairdos,
Low-cut dresses, high heels.
Enough of playing footsie under the table,
The meaningful look under the eye,

Licitiranja i rasprodaja:
Ko-će-kome, Ko-će-koga.

Dosta mi je vaših aperitiva i deserta
Mladih stršljenova i bezopasnih bumbara—
Vaših slatkih otrova.
Na smrt voljenih i ljubavi do kraja života.
Vašeg Sedmog neba što seže
Do vrhova Njegovih cipela.
I vitlejemskih jasli—Njegovog međunožja.
Dosta mi je, vašeg: «Po zeljama slusalaca».
Vaše *nevermore* stara je pesma,
Evergreen vaših kasnih proleća.
Sve bi dale za jednog muškarca
U liku bespomoćnog boga,
Vi Adamova rebarca.
Nemam ništa s vama.

Igračica bih da sam na trapezu,
Hodačica po žici, ukrotiteljica lavova.
Kroz obruč vatre bih da skočim
U svako grlo ili srce,
Da bih se ponovo rodila u porođajnim bolovima.
Sve bih isto a sve drukčije.
I Njegovu bih ljubljenu glavu
Na mom trbuhu—Salominom pladnju.

Auctions and bargain sales:
Who-will-do-what-to-whom.

Enough of you aperitifs and desserts.
Young studs and sugar daddies.
Your sweet poisons,
Loved to death till death do us part,
Your Seventh Heaven that rests
On the tip of His shoes.
Your Holy Mangers in the crotch of His legs.
Enough of your: "Our listeners request."
Your "nevermore" is an old song,
Evergreen of your late springs.
You'd give anything for a man
In the image of a helpless god,
Adam's rib.
I don't want anything more to do with you.

I'd like to be dancing on a trapeze,
Walking on high wire, taming lions.
Through a fiery hoop I'd jump
Into everyone's throat or heart,
So I can be born again in labor pains.
I'd do everything the same way and everything differently
With his beloved head on my belly—
As on Salome's plate.

PSALAM

Blagoslovena mašina za pranje veša, posuđa...
I ostali kućni aparati u ispravnom stanju.
Vodovod i kanalizacija. Uredna stolica.

Gradski saobraćaj i G-đa čistoća.
Blagosloveni—kiša i vetar,
Zanatlije, taksisti, trgovci. Novac.
Javna kupatila i narodne kuhinje.
Vrtlari i vidari mojih draži.
Grobari.

Sve što je na usluzi—blagosloveno:
Ustima, nozi, ruci. Zemlji.

Blagosloveni pokvareni telefoni,
Izgubljene adrese, pronađeni kišobrani.
Blagosloveni bivši prijatelji i ovdašnji
Neprijatelji. Dužni i sužnji. I ti,
Moj dragane, moja Euridiko.

Blagosloveni oni sportovi
Koji mi ne pođoše za rukom,
I društvene igre koje ne naučih.

Blagoslovene nepripitomljene životinje,
Ptice izletele iz kaveza, prazni kavezi,
I ti srce moje—ispražnjeni dućanu.

Sve oskudice i nestašice blagoslovene,
Što mi podariste svoje minute i sate;
Da zamišljam i gatam
Kao Ciganka nasred druma—
Za svaku reč zalažući svih 56 kg
Mesa sa kostima.

PSALM

Blessed are machines for washing laundry and dishes,
And other household appliances in working order.
Water and plumbing. Regular bowel movements.

Blessed are—wind and rain,
City traffic and Lady Sanitation.
Tradesmen, taxi drivers, merchants. Money,
Public baths and soup lines,
The spinners and healers of my distractions.
Gravediggers.

Everything that serves—the mouth,
The foot, the hand, the earth—is blessed.

Blessed are the telephones that are out of order,
Lost addresses, found umbrellas.
Blessed are ex-friends and today's
Enemies. The debtors and the incarcerated.
And you, my sweetheart, my Eurydice.

Blessed are the sports
For which I had no talent
And party games I never learned to play.

Blessed are the untamed beasts,
Birds that have flown out of a cage, empty cages,
And you my heart—a store with empty shelves.

All privations and shortages are blessed,
That gave me their minutes and their hours
To dream and to prophesy
Like a gypsy in the middle of the road
Vouching for every word with all of my 123 pounds
All of my meat and bones.

LETNJE NOĆI: SAMOĆA

Niko ne zove telefonom
I ne šapuće nežne reči.
Predveče ili u ponoć,
Kada zrikavci počnu
Nemilosrdno da zriču
Pojačavajući tišinu.

Kada sve postane gusto,
Kao ustajala krv—
Noć, i samoća svih stvari okolo.
Samo udari srca
Nadjačavaju gluvoću
Što se cedi niz kičmu, i naniže.
Kao znoj usred žege
I žudnja usred noći.

Budno i širom otvorenih očiju
Ležim u mraku,
Što ga ulične svetiljke uvećavaju,
I čine ne manje večnim.
Tu noć, taj mrak i samoću.

SUMMER NIGHT: SOLITUDE

No one calls on the phone
And whispers tender words,
At dusk or at midnight
When crickets commence
Chirping without pity
Intensifying the silence.

When everything thickens
Like sluggish blood—
Night and solitude of all things near.
Only the heart beats louder
Overpowering the numbness
Dripping down the spine and lower,
Like sweat during a heat wave
And burning desire in the night.

Awake with eyes wide open
I lie in the dark,
The streetlights enlarge
And make even more eternal.
That night, that dark, that solitude.

MINSKO POLJE

Za Čarlsa Simića

U nesreći nema veterana u mirovini,
Sa epoletama i tompusom u ustima,
U ležaljci za ljuljanje.
Obični smo redovi.
Vojnici bez činova i medalja,
Čije se vojevanje nikada ne završava.
Nema kupljenja prnja ni čaura,
Kao što nema ni objave rata.
Ne vrede pregovori, predaje,
Dizanje bele zastave.
Ali ni mašanje za pojas.
Vađenje pištolja ili hladnog oružja—
Biva samo pozorišni gest.
Pobeda se ne dovodi u pitanje,
Osim ako ispod grudne kosti
Ne sagradiš iglo od leda.
Što isključujem, odmah.

Odasvud tuče, iz svih topova.
Ne kriomice i noću,
Nego u po bela dan.
A najviše kad se najmanje nadaš.
Kad izuješ čizme,
Ili kad staneš pred ogledalo
Da se obriješ i zaližeš kosu
Za randevu s dragom,
Ma kako se ona zvala—
Helen, Rodni grad ili Poezija—samo.
Nema dopusta.
Nema na mestu voljno.
Ni posete salunima.
Točenja vina. Pijenje zaborava.
Ali ne vredi ni stalno marširanje,

MINEFIELD

For Charles Simic

In misfortune there are no pensioned-off veterans
With epaulets and big cigars in their mouths
Lying in a hammock.
We are just ordinary soldiers
Without rank or medals
Whose war never ends.
There are no rags and empty shells to gather,
Nor are there any declarations of hostilities.
No peace talks, surrenders,
The raising of the white flag,
Or reaching for the belt
Taking out a pistol or a knife—
All that is just theater,
The victory is never in doubt
Unless you build an igloo under your ribs
Which I very much doubt.

There's cannon fire from every direction,
Not stealthily at night
But in broad daylight,
Especially when you least expect it.
When you take off your boots
And stand before a mirror
To shave and comb your hair
For a date with some sweetheart,
Whatever her name is,
Helen, Native City or Poetry—only
There's no furlough,
No stand at ease,
No passes to visit the local saloons.
The pouring of wine. Drinking to forget.
Nor is constant marching of any use,
Sending scouts, lying in trenches.

Slanje izvidnice, ležanje u rovovima,
Sve to puzanje preko minskog polja!
Ni iskustvo bitaka—
Tek ono ne vredi, ni lule duvana!
Pronalazi nas svugde,
Bez durbina i bez raketnog navođenja.
I u mišjoj rupi.

Ne trepnuvši,
Sručuje u naš jastuk kišu metaka—
Kao da prosipa mesečinu,
Prosipa Judine srebrnjake
Iz izvrnutih džepova.
Pa ti sad hajde,
Zucni nešto o sreći,
O leptiru,vilin konjicu i buba-mari.
O Gospi sto s umećem spram sveća
Iglu svoju prodeva kroz tvoje srce.
Ili bar o Šelijevom sušičavom lišću
Koga tera zapadni vetar.

All that crawling over minefields!
Nor being toughened in battle—
That especially is not worth a damn!
It finds us anywhere
Without binoculars or missile-guiding systems,
In a mouse hole.

Without catching a wink,
It rains bullets into our pillow
As if it were pouring moonlight,
Pouring Judas's silver
Out of pockets turned inside out.
So now, let's hear you say
Something about happiness,
Butterflies, dragonflies or ladybugs,
Or the Virgin who deftly in candlelight
Threads her needle through your heart,
Or something about Shelley's dry leaves
The West Wind is scattering.

DUŠO...

Dušo, vidim ne mariš više ti za mene.
Moja pica beše tvoja amajlija,
Sad je više nećeš.

Oko druge suknje sad se motaš
U drugu zuriš i bleneš,
Pred njom šeniš kao štene.

Istina je,
Davila sam te kao žabu,
Pila sam ti krv kao pijavica.
A sad te je ćapila neka maca
Kao miša.
Smotala te je oko malog prsta.

Ali da znaš ne ridam za tobom
I ne cvilim—nekad bilo!
«Ostavi nju uzmi mene»—
Nije više moj refren.
Niko me više neće za nos vući,
Farbati.
Na kaišu kao pudlicu šetati.

Za tobom se više ne pretržem.
Na drugog sam oko bacila
Zašto kriti, kao maca već predem.
Sad smo kvit!

Ipak, ako te ona izgustira,
Ako te šutne, prevari s drugim...
Ne trči za njom i ne cvili,
Nego došepaj k meni,
I stopalo mi lizni.

DARLING

Darling, I can see you no longer care for me.
My pussy was your amulet.
Now you don't want it anymore.

Someone else's skirt keeps you close by.
At some other woman you stare and ogle,
Beg like a puppy in front of her.

The truth is, I strangled you
The way a snake does a frog,
I sucked your blood like a leech.
Now some cat snatched you
Like a mouse,
Tied you around her little finger.

If you want to know, I don't cry after you
And snivel—how it used to be!
"Leave her, take me"
Is no longer my refrain.
No one will lead me by the nose anymore,
Tell me fibs,
Walk me around on a leash like a poodle.

I don't jump at the thought of you.
I got my eye on another.
Why hide it, like a cat I'm purring already.
We are quits!

Still, if she grows weary of you.
Kicks you out, cheats on you…
Don't run after her and don't whine
But crawl right back to me
And lick my foot.

TAKVE PESME PIŠEM

Trebalo bi da imam novog ljubavnika,
Ovog da se ratosiljam
Kao konzerve kojoj je istekao rok upotrebe.

Trebalo bi brza kola da vozim
Kroz prozor kosa da mi vijori
Kao kod kakve Rozamunde
Što na konju jezdi.
Takve pesme pišem.

Trebalo bi do podne da spavam,
Da se izležavam na prostranom krevetu
Kao poleglo žito po «majčici» zemlji.

Trebalo bi da ne marim za vreme;
Da ne kaskam, da ne žurim.
Da ispijam dan za danom, do dna—naiskap!
Noć po noć, kao cigaretu za cigaretom.
Pa, opuške—pod potpeticu!
Reči na žar. Vrućicu u pesme.
Takve pesme pišem.

Trebalo bi usku haljinu da nosim.
Ramena krznom da ogrćem.
Visoke štikle na noge da natičem.
Da se nafrakam i nakinđurim,
Kao božićna jelka—
Da me ne prepozna ni rođena majka.

Trebalo bi da sam vedra, nasmejana, zavodljiva.
Da pevam i plešem do tri izjutra.
Da sam svesna svojih ženskih draži

THE POEMS I WRITE

I ought to have a new lover,
Get rid of the one I have
As if he were a can with a past-due date.

I ought to drive fast cars,
My hair flying out of the window
As if I were some Rosamund
Riding on a horse.
These are the poems I write.

I ought to sleep till noon,
Spread myself over a great big bed
Like wheat over "sweet mother" earth.

I ought not to care about time,
Not to move slowly, not to hurry,
To drink each day down to its dregs,
Night after night—like a chain-smoker—
And step on a butt with my heel.
Words are embers. I burn myself into poetry.
These are the poems I write.

I ought to wear tight dresses,
Drape my shoulders with furs,
Wear high heels on my heels,
Paint myself and cover myself with jewels
Like a Christmas tree—
So my own mother doesn't recognize me.

I ought to be cheerful, smiling, flirty,
To sing and dance till 3 A.M.
Mindful of my sex appeal

Kad mi kakav pastuv pride.
Takve pesme pišem.

Trebalo bi da me ne dotiču
Žaoke, bodlje, bumbara i osa.
Maramicom kao kap znoja sa čela
Da obrišem svaku boru, brigu.

Trebalo bi da imam dovoljno love
Za kiriju, porez i još pride.
Lova dobro dođe kad ponestane ostaloga.
Kad zature se poljupci, kad iscure reči.
S lovom mogu disati na kredit!

Trebalo bi telo svoje da sunčam
Na nekoj steni,
Daleko od dokova Sunovrata.
Trebalo bi iz zemlje Apatije
U zemlju Želja da emigriram.
Sve da želim ničeg da se ne odričem.
Trebalo bi u mirišljavoj peni da se kupam
Žilet veni da primičem.
Takve pesme pišem.

When some stud approaches me.
These are the poems I write.

Thorns, bumblebees and bees with their stingers
Ought not to touch me.
With my handkerchief I'll wipe every worry and wrinkle
As if they were drops of sweat on my forehead.

I ought to have enough dough
For rent, taxes and a few more things.
Money comes in handy when there's nothing else.
When kisses are misplaced, when words all trickle out.
With money one can breathe on credit.

I ought to tan my body on some rock
Far from the piers of Disaster.
I ought to emigrate from the land of Apathy
To the land of Wishes
So I can desire all and renounce nothing.
I ought to bathe myself in scented bubbles,
Draw a razor to my vein.
These are the poems I write.

BIĆU OPAK BABAC

Vidim biću opak babac
Mršava kao pljoska,
Kao i sad što sam.
Ne od onih debelguzih
Što valjaju za sobom zadnjice,
Kako veli Selin.
Ne od onih dobroćudnih baba-tetaka
Uz čije je meke i punačke mišice
Lepo prisloniti obraz.
Više nalik onim strašilima za ptice
U našim baštama
Punim rumenih paradajza
Kao dečijih obraza.
Ima takvih bakutanera
Živahnih i ljutih kao osice
Sa očima navrh čela,
Sve vide, sve čuju, i imaju primedbe.
Gunđala od rođenja.
Zvocaću i torokaću povazdan.
Kokodakaću kao kvočka pilićima
O vremenima kada bejah
Mlada i zgodna cura,
I kada momke vrteh oko malog prsta,
Ždrepce i pastuve dok krotila sam,
Sevom oka, sevom suknje.
Prećutkujući sva neverstva
I sve jade, kao izgubljene bitke general.
Kao bapcu sve će mi biti dozvoljeno
Od onoga što mogu i želim,
Da igram bridž i da plešem
Okretne igre moga doba.
Okretaću se i saplitati
O sopstvene štapičaste noge,

I'LL BE A WICKED OLD WOMAN

I'll be a wicked old woman
Thin as a rail,
The way I am now.
Not one of those big-assed ones
With buttocks churning behind them,
As Celine said.
Not one of the good-natured grandmas and aunties
Against whose soft and plump arms
It is nice to lay one's cheek.
I'm more like a scarecrow
In our gardens full of rosy tomatoes
Like children's cheeks.
There are some old crones
Who are both vivacious and angry as a bee
With eyes on top of their heads
Who see everything, hear everything and have an opinion—
Grumblers since birth.
I'll squawk and chatter all day,
Cackle like a hen over her chicks
About the days when I was
A young, good-looking girl,
When I led boys by the nose.
Colts and stallions I tamed
With the flash in my eye, the flash of my skirt.
Passing over infidelities and miseries
The way a general passes over his lost battles.
I'll be free to do anything as an old woman,
Among things I still can and want to do
Like playing bridge or dancing
The light-footed dances of my days.
I'll spin and trip on my sticklike legs,
Attached to my body like toothpicks to a kabob.

Udenute u trup kao čačkalice u ćevap.
Bakutaner i po!
Klicaće i aplaudiraće mi,
Mladi pametnjakovići skupljeni oko mene.
Bakuta kao reš kifla sa susamom—
Takva ću biti,
Svakom zapadaću za zube, kao i ranije—
Dok sa velikim šeširom i haljinom do poda
Budem šetala po predlima bivšeg života,
Mirišući žutilovku, diveći se vresu,
O svaki čičak zakačinjući podsuknju-dušu.

That old hag sure can boogie!
The young smarties gathered around me
Will shout and applaud.
An old woman like a well-baked bun with sesame seeds,
That's what I'm going to be like.
I'll stick between everyone's teeth, as I did before,
While with a wide hat and dresses down to the ground
I stroll through landscapes of my past life.
Smelling the furze, admiring the heather,
On every thistle catching my undergarment—my soul.

URUŠAVANJE

Šta je ostalo od tebe:
Oplata, kreč, zidovi što se krune,
Naprsle grede?
Pod koji ne može da izdrži
Moju težinu: stopala, nutrinu?

Krckaš i škripiš—ječiš,
Pri svakom mom pokretu.
Oprosti ne umem da hodam na prstima,
Ne umem da hodam na rukama,
Da dubim na glavi.
Da lebdim i lepršam
Potrebno je više od krila—
Da se odvojim od tela.

Priznajem, tapkam u mestu, ali ne zadugo.
Od zmijskog sam soka
I kad milim žalac bacam.
Nadahnjuje me boja tvoga lica—
Boja uprljanog zida,
Loše opranog veša.

Hoćeš tanjirić mleka?
Ali nema više, nema!
Nema kuće. Nema krova—oduvala sam ga.
Oduvala tvoju rukotvorinu,
Tvoje remek delo ljubavi i čarobnjaštva,
Dizano-spuštano po tvojoj meri—
Kao sečivo nad mojom glavom.

Sad je i poslednji crep spao,
Skljokao ti se na glavu—odrubljenu.
I ja nebo vidim—obećanu zemlju,
Ali tražiti te tamo neću.

GOING TO RUIN

What remained of you:
Weather stripping, lime, peeling walls,
Cracked beams?
The floor that won't bear
My weight, the soles of my feet, my innards?

You creak and squeak—whimper
At my every movement.
Forgive me, I don't know how to walk on my toes,
Don't know how to walk on my hands,
To stand on my head.
To hover and flutter—
I need more than two wings
To separate myself from my body.

I admit, I stamp my feet, but not for long.
I'm of a serpent's breed.
Even when I crawl I flick my tongue.
The color of your face inspires me—
Color of a dirtied wall, badly washed laundry.

Do you want a saucer of milk?
There's none to be had anymore, none!
There's no house, no roof—I blew it all away,
Blew the work of your hands,
Your masterpiece of love and magic.
Raised and lowered to your measure
Like a blade over my head.

Now the last roof tile has fallen,
Fallen on your head—and chopped it off.
Now I can see the sky—the promised earth,
But I won't look for you there.

TAMO, OVDE

Ostrvce do koga nikada ne doplovih,
Niti doplivah.
Ostrvce na koje nikada ne kročih—
Mišljah biće vremena.
Ne tako udaljeno,
Reklo bi se na dohvat,
Gledasmo sa obale, sa spruda,
I zastavši—
Uvek pri povratku sa plaže,
Danima dok god tu boravismo.

Jegulje, rakovi, lenjost.
Čak i zagrljaji. Naizmeničan meni!
Samo je ono bilo stalno, nepromenjeno.
Titralo na sunčevoj izmaglici.
Čekalo ukotvljeno,
Mameć na ne odveć veliku avanturu.

Ushićen njegovom lepotom,
Jednog predvečerja, ti ga nazva
Nekakvim literarnim imenom—
Kojeg sada ne mogu da se setim.
I sve se završi na tome.
Odosmo u žurbi.
Šta beše razlog, ko bi sad to znao?!

I godinama potom,
Dok se davismo u zaboravu,
Ono je izranjalo iz ničijih voda.
Iz plavozelenog. Nedirnuto.
I gnezda galebova i zmija.
I zatoni. I puste plaže s njim.

THERE, HERE

The island I never swam to,
Or sailed to.
The island I never stepped on—
I thought there'd be plenty of time.
It's not far,
Almost within reach,
We saw it from the shore, from the sandbar,
Dillydallying—
While returning from the beach
In days when we came here.

Eels, crabs, laziness.
Even embraces. Taking turns!
Only the island remained the same,
Shimmering in the sun-haze—
Waiting, anchored like a ship,
Tempting one on not-so-great an adventure.

Ecstatic before its beauty,
One evening you called it
By some literary name
Which I cannot recall now.
And it all ended with that,
We left in a hurry.
Who can remember for what reason?

Years afterwards
While we drowned in forgetfulness,
The island rose from the blue-green
Waters belonging to no one. Intact.
And the nests of seagulls and snakes,
And sunsets. And the empty beaches.

I naša tela
Koja nikada ne legoše tamo,
Behu opružena jedno kraj drugoga
Na letnjoj žezi, gotovo bestelesna,
Isprana od zapljuskivanja talasa
Žudnje i sećanja—

Kao na tanjiru
Kosturi onih oglodanih jegulja,
I sada leže tamo ostavljena.

A i ovde nisu bolja.

And our bodies, which had never
Lain there, stretched out
One next to the other
In summer heat, almost ethereal,
Washed by the splashing waves,
Desire and memories—

Like gnawed eel bones
On a plate,
They are still lying there.

And here, too, they are like that.

MOJ ČOVA

«Večiti dečko»,
Tako se zove rod kome pripada.
Prešao je pedesetu.
Teme mu je pista za lake letilice.
Trbuščić mu kipi preko kaiša kao testo.
Ali sve to nema veze s njim!
Mlade curice—slatke pilulice,
Guta pogledom,
I okreće se za njima kao navijen ringišpil.

Radi se o takvom primerku
Čiji se pimpek sve više klati
Kao prerezana kokošija šija
Ili prebijena pseća šapa.
Ali to nema veze s njim!
Treba ga samo držati obema rukama
Milovati ga i tepati mu,
Kao da se radi o ratnom invalidu
Koji nije dobio zaslužen orden,
Pa mu ga morate dati ovoga časa.
Što neizostavno i činim.

Radi se o takvom primerku roda,
Do čijeg srca vodi slepa ulica.
O takvom primerku,
Koga nikad ne vidite izjutra
U svom ogledalu
Sa penom za brijanje na licu.
O takvom primerku,

MY FELLOW

"The eternal child"
Is the name of species to which he belongs.
He's over fifty.
The back of his head is a landing strip for small aircraft.
His belly boils over his belt like dough.
But all that doesn't matter!
Young babes—sweet pills,
He swallows with his eyes
And turns after them like a merry-go-round.

The type I have in mind
Whose prick dangles more and more
Like a severed chicken neck
Or a broken dog's paw—
But all that doesn't matter!
All it needs is to be held in both hands,
Stroked and sweet-talked
As if he were a disabled veteran
Who never got that well-earned medal,
So he needs to get it now,
Which I immediately oblige.

The type I have in mind,
To whose heart one takes a dead-end street,
The type one never sees
In one's mirror in the morning
With shaving cream on his face,
The one who is like worn goods

Iznošenom kao roba iz Second Hand-a.
Ali s mojim čovom to nema veze!

Moje srce igra
Kao Džinđžer Rođžers i Fred Aster,
Čim ga ugledam.

In a Salvation Army store.
But all that has nothing to do with my fellow!

My heart dances
Like Ginger Rodgers and Fred Astaire,
When I see him coming.

POSLEDNJE PUTOVANJE: NEW YORK—BEOGRAD

Ko mi je to pričao i gde?
Da su njegovu urnu,
Tj. ono što je ostalo od njega,
Prokrijumčarili avionom iz New York-a.
Donela ga je u svojoj tašni prijateljica.

Stavila ga je međ lične stvari,
Uz dokumenta, novčanik, šminku,
Svežnjeve ključeva i koješta još,
Maramice, uloške, tampone.

Držala ga je u krilu, na kolenima,
Onako kako inače žene drže tašne
Pridržavajući ih obema rukama,
I stiskajući ih u sebe
Kadgod ih uhvati san.

Tako je činila i ona.
Svog ga je obujmila rukama,
Tj. ono što je ostalo od njega,
Takoreći grlila je,
Ono što je već bilo samo uspomena:
Bivši školski drug, bivši prijatelj,
Bivša ljubav, bivši taj i taj.

Do juče beskućan kao toliki.
Sad je ležao u njenom krilu,
Na sigurnom.
Na njenim butinama,
Možda toplim, možda mekim.
Nije se dalo proveriti.

LAST VOYAGE: NEW YORK—BELGRADE

Who told me that and where?
That they took his urn,
With what was left of him,
Snuck it by plane from New York,
Had a friend bring him in her purse.

She put him between her things,
Documents, wallet, makeup,
Key rings and all kinds of other things,
Handkerchiefs, insoles, sanitary napkins.

Kept him in her lap, on her knees,
The way women usually hold purses
With both hands,
Pressing them against themselves
When they happen to doze off.

That's what she did too.
She wrapped her arms around
All that was left of him,
Almost embracing
What was already only a memory:
Old school friend, ex-friend,
Former lover, former so-and-so.

Till yesterday homeless like so many others,
Now sitting in her lap,
On her dependable
Perhaps warm, perhaps soft thighs.
There's no way to find out.

On her bare knees
That stuck out noticeably

Na njenim golim kolenima
Što su poprilično provirivala
Ispod suknje koju je nosila.
Ali, avaj!
U ovom stanju
Ni krišom ih nije mogao pogledati.

Putovao je u svoju rodnu zemlju
Kao nikada dotad.
U onu zemlju
U koju se njeni građani vraćaju
Kao slepi putnici, kao on sada—
Bez sanjarenja i bez suza.
Kao teglice pomade
Ili pudrijere u tuđim tašnama.

Under the skirt she wore.
Which, alas!
In the state he was in
He couldn't peek under.

As never before,
He was on his way home
To a country
Whose citizens return
Like blind travelers
Without daydreams, without tears.
Like jars of hand cream
Or compacts in strangers' purses.

RADMILA LAZIĆ, born in 1949, is one of the best living Serbian poets. She is the author of six collections of poetry, for which she received several literatry prizes. She has published numerous essays on literature and is the editor of an anthology of women's poetry and another of anti-war letters, and the founder and editor of the journal *Profemina*. These are the first translations of her poetry into English.

CHARLES SIMIC is a poet, essayist, and translator. He has published sixteen collections of his own poetry, five books of essays, a memoir, and numerous books of translations, for which he has received many literary awards including the PEN Translation Award. His collection of prose poems, *The World Doesn't End,* won the 1990 Pulitzer Prize. He teaches American literature and creative writing at the University of New Hampshire. *The Voice at 3:00 A.M.,* his selected and new poems, was recently published.

The text of this book has been set in Adobe Garamond, drawn by
Robert Slimbach and based on type cut by Claude Garamond in the
sixteenth century.

Book design by Wendy Holdman.
Composition by Stanton Publication Services, Inc., St. Paul, Minnesota.
Manufactured at Thomson-Shore on acid-free paper.